WHAT TO EAT, WHAT TO DRINK, WHAT TO LEAVE FOR POISON

What to Eat, What to Drink, What to Leave for Poison

poetry

C AMILLE T. D UNGY

R ED H EN P RESS   L OS A NGELES

What to Eat, What to Drink, What to Leave for Poison

Cover art: "Southern Woman" by James Denmark
        24" x 30", collage. 1999

Book design by Michael Vukadinovich
Cover design by Mark E. Cull
Author Photo by DeWardrick Mack

ISBN: 1-59709-000-X
Library of Congress Catalog Card Number: 2001012345

Red Hen Press
www.redhen.org

The City of Los Angeles Cultural Affairs Department, California Arts Council, Los Angeles County Arts Commission and National Endowment for the Arts partially support Red Hen Press.

First edition

my family in spirit and in blood, this book, with love, is for you

ACKNOWLEDGEMENTS

Poems in the manuscript have appeared or are forthcoming in the following publications:

"Language" and "First Fire" (as "At Ten") in *Weber Studies*; "How Quickly He Went," "Before My History Classes," "Vo-Tech" (reprinted on *Poetry Daily*), "From Someplace," "In His Library," and "Lament" in *The Missouri Review*; "Concordance" in *Beloit Poetry Journal*; "Depression" and "What You Want" in *Hotel Amerika*; "Visiting Springfield in Winter" in *32 Poems*; "Requiem" on www.fishousepoems.org; "black spoon" in *Brilliant Corners* (reprinted on www.fishousepoems.org); "Jacob's Ladder, Jacob Lawrence," in *Obsidian III* and in *Image/Word: A Book of Poems*; "Black Boy," "Here's $100, cause I'll be coming back the other way," and "Greyhound to Baton Rouge" in *Warpland: A Journal of Black Literature and Ideas*; "Got" in *Ekphrasis*; "We were two rooms of one timber, but I left that place alone," "Farm Bureau Advisor" (reprinted on the NEA Writers' Corner website), "Free Masons at the Door," and "Service Station, Tennessee" in *The Southern Review*; "How She Didn't Say It" in *Cave Canem VI, Anthology 2001*; "The Abattoir" in *Caketrain*; "To Put Things Right" in *Cider Press Review*; "How It Happened," in *Sou'Wester*; "Fear" in *The Louisville Review*; "Ark" in *Melic Review*; "My Grandmother Takes the Youth Group to Services," in *HerMark 2003*, Woman Made Gallery; "Cleaning" in *Crab Orchard Review*; "The Preachers Eat Out" (reprinted on www.fishousepoems.org), and "After Applying to Harvard, Colgate, Yale" (reprinted on the NEA Writers' Corner website) in *Mid-America Review*; "What to Eat, and What to Drink, and What to Leave for Poison" in *The Midwest Quarterly*.

The writing of many of these poems has been supported by fellowships from the National Endowment for the Arts, The Virginia Center for the Creative Arts, the Rocky Mountain National Park Artist-in-Residence Program, The Ragdale Foundation, The Corporation of Yaddo, A Room of One's Own Foundation, The Norton Island/Eastern Frontier Society, and the Cave Canem Foundation, as well as the Tennessee Williams Scholarship at the Sewanee Writers Workshop, and the John Atherton Scholarship at the Bread Loaf Writers' Conference.

What to Eat, What to Drink, What to Leave for Poison benefited from the support, care, and critical eyes of many readers, teachers, and friends including Tayari A. Jones, V. Penelope Pelizzon, Shara McCallum, Jane Satterfield, Tara Powell, William Logan, Laura-Gray Street, Matt O'Donnell, Lola Haskins, Tyehimba Jess, Aviya Kushner, Reetika Vazirani, Emily Warn, Jim Peterson, Marilyn Nelson, my Cave Canem family, and my own dear family: Dr. Claibourne I. Dungy, Dr. Madgetta T. Dungy, Dr. Edgar T. Thornton, Dr. Madge Thornton, Jesse W. Dungy, Euphemia Mickens Dungy, Dr. Kathryn R. Dungy, and Jesse L. Dungy. I thank you all for your consistent support, your dedication to poetry, and your insistence that this book find its own best way to honor the word.

Contents

WHAT TO EAT, WHAT TO DRINK, WHAT TO LEAVE FOR POISON

LANGUAGE

Silence is one part of speech, the war cry
of wind down a mountain pass another.
A stranger's voice echoing through lonely
valleys, a lover's voice rising so close
it's your own tongue: these are keys to cipher,
the way the high hawk's key unlocks the throat
of the sky and the coyote's yip knocks
it shut, the way the aspens' bells conform
to the breeze while the rapid's drums define
resistance. Sage speaks with one voice, pinyon
with another. Rock, wind her hand, water
her brush, spells and then scatters her demands.
Some notes tear and pebble our paths. Some notes
gather: the bank we map our lives around.

UNDER THE BLUE FLAME . . .

How Quickly He Went

Even at eighty-five he might have lived
twenty-five more years if he could have hoped
the wife who pulled away from him and stayed
on that station platform down in Springfield
might still change her mind. It was his desire
for her that had staked him forty years. Love
was one slim woman with a nursing job
in Illinois. Life was a small business,
a Gary tailor shop he could not sell
until the war ended...the note was paid...
until all chance with her had passed. She died
in February. Before October
slung shivers on the wind, he stopped breathing.
What was the use of holding some body?

CONCORDANCE

It is nineteen forty-seven. Somewhere
in Pittsburgh steel spits in a cooling tank.
Somewhere in Gary iron curves toward flame.
And, this could be anywhere, a woman
reconsiders his final letter, marks
with her finger welts the sentences left
on the page. Outside it is December.
Her garden is a crop of stone. We have
language to describe a woman like this.
Even in summer her tomatoes grow
yellow-skinned and rock-hearted. She will keep
her windows closed even under the blue
flame of August days. We have many terms
that define distance. We might say once, when
she was a thin-necked girl, one man collapsed
the many intricacies of heaven
into the four syllables it took to spell
her name. There must be a phrase that explains this
desire. She questions her response. Did she
read his plan right? Somewhere in Milwaukee
men stir hops and thirst for sweet abandon.
When she was a slim-fingered girl no ring
suited her taste. We have plenty of words
to describe a woman like that. But now,
since she followed the tracks laid in his eyes?
Her whole life a coupled string of freight
and rusting emptiness? Those children waving,
running beside her through the sun-scorched yard?

Before My History Classes

I had religion on my mind and knew
questions would stall my Mother when she came
to tuck the starched, white sheet under my chin.

I wanted to be older, to be free
like my sister who wore black leather pumps
and stayed awake as late as grown ups did.
I wasn't a little kid anymore.

I tricked Mom into talking about Christ,
the Bible, and what Heaven held in store.
Why should I sleep? I told her, *When I die
I want to meet all the dead. They'll be dressed
and acting just like they did when they lived.*

She snapped the sheet, a warning, kissed my head.
Someday you'll be more careful what you wish.

DEPRESSION

What little he brought home wouldn't buy much
happiness—a chicken to hem trousers
and some eggs to take them in four inches
at the waist. Hell, it wouldn't even buy
milk. He had time enough to stitch his wife
the only tailored dish towels in town,
so he knew only she could keep the house
around them. A nurse will always find work.

What had he provided since their wedding?
The dream of a trip to the Falls; passports
for Canada; a suitcase; a marriage
certificate; all that useless paper—
five hundred dollars, traveler's checks (all
his money) drawn on a Friday-failed bank.

Vo-Tech

Everything we wore that needed rescue,
pants we'd torn and shirts with ripped off buttons,
went to our Grandpa when we visited.
We modeled while he adjusted our hems.
Because he loved us, he tried to save us,
my sister and me, by restoring clothes
we'd lately damaged. *You should teach the girls
how this is done,* Mother once suggested,
her arms delivering mending, her eyes
collecting Grandpa's hands, the snapped-tight box
that housed his machine, his needles. He ripped
her words as he told us never to do
to a hanging thread. *Let them save their time.*
He took the clothes. *Let them do useful things.*

Pity

Christ bore what suffering he could and died
a young man, but you waited years to learn
how to heal. Only when you could did you
touch the man whose body blistered for yours.

You posted him no news for sixteen terms,
then just a signed graduation notice.

The letter he wrote that week asked only,
Now that your books are closed, can boys come in?

At your wedding, you buried the woman
you thought you knew inside a stranger's name.

This is how you found yourself: thirty-three,
nursing a son. Soon there was another.
Your mind had already begun to walk.
But you were a mother. Those cribs held you.

FROM SOMEPLACE

Dreams are sometimes livable, provided
there is property enough, and each house
in Buxton had a little plot of land.
All the town's employees had a garden,
and black folks grew theirs right among the whites'.
A Negro could make a life in Buxton,
and Great-grandfather, the village's best
blacksmith, did. His daughter was free to pass
any old place. This is the youth you knew,
and why you knew, years, miles later, you'd leave
the blackening mill town of your marriage.
You found a town with promise, moved your sons
to its white district, wouldn't let them swim
in the mud hole they called the colored pool.

APPEARANCES

I.

She was meticulous, my uncle said,
your grandmother. Except one late morning
she left home too quickly. The wrinkled hem
of her nurse's whites revealed her slip's lace
and flashed glimpses of St. John Hospital's
only colored thighs. Doctors never came
so close to touching her before. She felt
her crumpled hem and translated the lust
that raised their smiles. At home her boys would learn
to iron. She said they should have warned her.
Yes, boys, like that. A seam should always stand
at attention. That, loves, is the reason
for family. We must guard each other.
We must make sure we always look our best.

II.
In boot camp my uncle kept heavy wire,
and when bivouacking he hung his clothes
so his uniform dropped stink and wrinkles.
One kid in his unit teased everyone.
During maneuvers he might watch his face
reflected in the rifle he cradled:
Look at me, he'd grin, I'm Dungy, crawling
a trench and worried about my collar.
My uncle wormed the floor, showed me how low
bodies had to be to clear those hazards:
Boot camp, but live ammunition. Rockets
unhinged the boy and made his body rise.
That arched back, his final insult. No one,
my uncle said, had the time to warn him.

In His Library

Grandpa's wife lived in Springfield. I suppose
that's why he collected those books I read
about the *Great Emancipator's* life,
but hope meant little to me in those days.

The best book proved *villains* could be *vanquished*,
and photos lent support. Conspirators,
friends of John Wilkes Booth, hung. Their hooded heads
all the evidence I needed. My folks
bored me, so I read while they asked Grandpa
if he planned to join his wife in Springfield.

*It's not but a few years since lynch mobs ran
that town. What good's Springfield ever done me?*

At eight, what did I know of frustration?
I read the book. That's what we call learning.

FIRST FIRE

Stripped in a flamedance, the bluff backing our houses
quivered in wet-black skin. A shawl of haze tugged tight
around the starkness. We could have choked on August.

Smoke thick in our throats, nearly naked as the earth,
we played bare feet over the heat caught in asphalt.
Could we, green girls, have prepared for this? Yesterday,

we played in sand-carpeted caves. The store we built
sold broken bits of ice plant, empty snail shells, leaves.
Our school's walls were open sky. We reeled in wonder

from the hills, oblivious to the beckoning
crescendo and to our parent's hushed communion.
When our bluff swayed into the undulation, we ran

into the still streets of our suburb, feet burning
against a fury that we did not know was change.

VISITING SPRINGFIELD IN WINTER

Camphor steam followed my older sister
when she came outside to play. I showed her
icicles, then we tossed snowballs. Except
when I had to say hello then goodbye
to the coughing woman, limp flesh on blue
bedding, I'd spent the day studying snow.

I had some questions, but I had no words
to speak to the woman. No words to ask
my father, who drove home, fast and silent,
through the tail-lit night, if she was someone
I should love. On the road, we hit black ice.
Our tilt-a-whirl sent me into giggles
until I caught, thrown from Dad's orphaned eyes,
a freezing thing I'd never touched before.

LAMENT

Those black men flew out of Tuskegee armed
with trades, and that diploma oversaw
his store. Now there's nothing but the mirror
in our basement and an oak spool-holder,
a plaque of thread my mother still consults
when she mends a hem. My father's father
is a photo I barely recognize.
He lives in my uncle's face. He reaches
for me with my father's hands, but he died
before I knew anything about him
but cast-off things, died before I could write
a story for him about anything
but loss. What do I know if I don't know
what it is that would have made him a man?

where jasmine lemon-sweets wind and salt
slicks the breeze   where sage spices sundrench
there   where the fragrant cloud-nest drives
the pump-beat of my blood   I am home.

long time gone.   long time gone and don't know
when I'm coming back   but see me there.
where the orange tree blossoms and the sky
smells white as line-dried sheets   see me there.

where jasmine lemon-sweets wind and salt
slicks the hair you wear into the breeze.
where cactus fruit is suckling pear
and its sweet-hidden water's everywhere
I am home.   am gone   but I'll be back.
long time gone.   but I'll be coming back.

SWING OUT ON MY ROAD . . .

REQUIEM

> Sing the mass—
> light upon me washing words
> now that I am gone.

The sky was a hot, blue sheet the summer breeze fanned
out and over the town. I could have lived forever
under that sky. Forgetting where I was,
I looked left, not right, crossed into a street
and stepped in front of the bus that ended me.

Will you believe me when I tell you it was beautiful—
my left leg turned to uselessness and my right shoe flung
some distance down the road? Will you believe me
when I tell you I had never been so in love
with anyone as I was, then, with everyone I saw?

The way an age-worn man held his wife's shaking arm,
supporting the weight that seemed to sing from the heart
she clutched. Knowing her eyes embraced the pile
that was me, he guided her sacked body through the crowd.
And the way one woman began a fast the moment she looked

under the wheel. I saw her swear off decadence.
I saw her start to pray. You see, I was so beautiful
the woman sent to clean the street used words
like police tape to keep back a young boy
seconds before he rounded the grisly bumper.

The woman who cordoned the area feared my memory
would fly him through the world on pinions of passion
much as, later, the sight of my awful beauty pulled her down
to tears when she pooled my blood with water
and swiftly, swiftly washed my stains away.

BLACK SPOON

Billie Holiday

baby you were meant to be home   you were
meant to be what I ain't never known   blue flame
done melted my song and you won't tell me
if you'll risk the curse between my thighs
won't give me more than the music of your fingers
strumming my slip's strap   your chest sings
to my heart's ear while your wicked wisdom works
its secret privilege   but you won't give me more
than your body tuned for walking out my door
hush now   I'm the one done let you in
here's what I've been cooking   what I scored
before you came   you brought me nothing
I ain't already known   I'm bright as a horn
listen   I'll blow you down

ANNUNCIATION

Perhaps in the peace of her dreams
her skin is the skin of unharvested fruit. Flesh not worth

thorns. Perhaps she dreams no sparrow,
no lark's beak, no clasped and unclasped hands will seek her, withered,

wrinkled as she is. In truth, she has lived through the dying
of men children and virgin hope, but she has never been

an old woman. Never anything but young. Like the queen
whose body is renewed each day in someone else's blood,

as if suffering were the secret source of youth. She wakes
and understands the passion cries that draw her young body

are nothing but the high sounds of her name. Year after year
Mary will remain just the girl

we expect. All through the ages she'll remain. The girl with
only one dream worth repeating.

Jacob's Ladder, Jacob Lawrence

Jacob understood
his dream. He had

to build himself a stairwell
to raise himself to God. Jacob

understood this much: The artist
comes last in all things unless he wins

his right from those who stand before him.
There can be no knowing where he deceived.

Lest a voice bring down his art, he shaded his truth.
Red bright bows to his command. His gray shines, steeling

barbs. He golds the thick smell of game-full fields, and he black
furs over what was white and smooth. He will conjure for the wretched

blind a vision. He will call a blessing down upon himself. For who would not
give over the whole world just to watch this Jacob? To watch this Jacob make it new.

BLACK BOY

Richard Wright

The beginning was only loneliness
aching long and into script. It served me
so well I would not call it grief. You see
what I have become? This, then, is something
like an answer. It fed me. How could I
call it pain? Do not regret the mortar
if the wall's built well.

                          Speculation won't
win you wisdom, friend. You still want to know
what I pray? That is all you want to know.
What do I ask of God? Give me a book
they will talk well about forever?

                            Books.
Who is in them who can touch me? My books,
my house, my hopes, my heart, all these I owe
to nothing. Give me anything but that.

WHAT YOU WANT

There is a kind of woman whose switch
comes from the willow of her hair
and whose sway is unnerving
and who branches what she knows
and whom
far beyond your knowing.

A kind of woman miraculous as the flight
of many heavy birds. You crane to see her
formation shifting always in and again in
to a darting perfection that knows where heat lives.

Her kettle is ever brewing
and inside you will find bits of yourself
skin and muscle and force of will
slipping off the bone   tender   and delicious.

Got

After Jean Dubuffett's Fugitive

She was liquid, moved like the billows
        and wet my skin. Liquid.
                I bought time
for loving her. Was a day way way back

I wouldn't touch her. She was so clear
        she slid on down whatever,
                slid on down
like something other, and never had to be

nowhere, nothing she didn't want. Seemed to me
        there must be something
                wrong
with a woman had that kind of freedom.

She was liquid, poured, couldn't stop her, down
        and out despite the cup my hands
                would hold her in.
Gone if she wanted. Anywhere

at all. But all this hot heat pulled her my way
        with the moon.
                So here I am now,
here I absolutely am. It's a flood all around me,

water every single where. And ain't no pumping I can do
        to free and clear myself.
                No running away
from her kind of holding tight. Until she pulls

the other way, tossing me from sleep to the dirt
        of just my body there to hold,
                    until she leaves me
dreaming, oh to touch her, oh to touch her running over me.

SINNER, DON'T YOU WEEP

This was before shame, before the word
for nakedness. The world was little matter.

We were just two bodies in the night.
In that old place death was no more

brutal than the sea I dove in everyday. I was light
floating over water. There was no word yet

for soiled.   Salt jeweled my skin and I
sucked the dark taste of my pleasure.

Do not tell me you do not understand.
I have seen your eyes lap, known your skin

to swallow what another's skin has shed.
I have watched you drink a body. Do not

tell me you are innocent of hunger. Desire
is the flesh, the fruit you cry for every night.

WE WERE TWO ROOMS OF ONE TIMBER, BUT I LEFT THAT PLACE ALONE
Sara, widow, 31

Henry pulled our heartwood along the rutted street
that town stood beside, built two rooms
and called them home. My Henry did that.
There. And I lived all those days inside his love.

But there is a kind of hunger that feeds
on flesh. Only, let it be yearning, heaving,
rising flesh. Only, let it be flesh living
and loving. Alive. Let it be life.
There is a kind of hunger that feeds on life.

They carved into him with banquet knives,
made stew of his skin and stirred it
with his own bones. My Henry served: the meat
and the pot to cook it in. And there was no charge
against the men who made that meal.

How She Didn't Say It

It used to bother me when people I didn't know
called me Ella   they ain't been blue   no
they should say Miss Fitzgerald   somehow
they never do   you have to let them see
the sweat   just don't let them see the feeling
stealing down below the ground you walk   listen
to the voice Chick said   he said don't look
at her   their eyes close and I'm rising up
Sinatra at my feet like I'm his friend   his
wet nurse   Tormé calling me Ella   Ella   I'm called
into nights I don't recognize   my song
like a cashbox   no change in their hearts
but I'm up here already   have to do something
my voice passes through them   shining   a knife

THE ABATTOIR

Who was he to think that because we were once friends,
before the glasses, and the neck-gear, and the growth
so fast even his new clothes hung short, that we would
risk the shoot of laughter dropping us beside him?

Who was he to think his gentle invitations,
the dance his father risked some real embarrassment
to afford, could inspire our mercy? We were
butchers, knives unsheathed, our cleavers at the ready.
We were young and strong and starving. That thing, that bone

and skin and meat behind the altar? Just one boy
went, because he had to go. His mother drove him
to the temple and watched him walk inside. But us?
The winter of adolescence was upon us.
Who was he to think his was a life we would spare?

To Put Things Right

What I saw first was an elephant rising,
and though the sight was glorious, it was not
half so decadent as other feasts offered up
that day—women robed in flame wishing
through air toward men in hats as tall as I
on legs as tall as father who held hoops
through which the women sped before arrowing,
violent and graceful as phoenix, into a pool
and streaming out, one, two, three, four, five
spangled flyers from one, two, three, four,
even five corners of the cornerless pool,
into our thick applause—so that I let go
her rising and fed my eyes to gluttony.

But it is that first sight I would sip up

had I to choose just one of my lives
to live again. The first crunch of sawdust
beneath my feet, her knees. Popcorn stalled
between my hand and mouth. There was meal enough
in the sight of her rising. First, just her
on her knees, skin char-gray under those glares—
even her naked hairs showing—and then her rising;
the earth shifted forward under the press of her knees,
and I tilted with it, we all tilted forward, so she could rise
ever so slowly (we heard trust in her heaves of breath),
and we were not breathing; an elephant stumbled,
we understood, as anyone might, we swallowed;
and then her rising, and the world put right,
and women, robed in flame, wishing through air.

How It Happened

O.J.

Between the field and heaven all they saw
was a black man with disappearing legs
and arms more secure than God's. They saw me
just the way they wanted, and they were bound
to worship me. What could they do but pay
to watch me move? All those people, bodies
shouting my name, I became somebody
they remembered, someone they had to love.
On Sundays I poured into their houses
while they guzzled the liquid of my speed,
and so I multiplied the bread. I ran.
I ran so far with what Ferguson passed
everybody knew I couldn't be stopped.
I was so fast I even beat myself.

HERE'S $100, 'CAUSE I'LL BE COMING
BACK THE OTHER WAY
Jack Johnson

There are men you can stop, some you can slow,
but I'm neither. And this car, it isn't
even a hint of what makes me so fast
some kid-glove wielding bulk of white men's pride
couldn't hope to knock stillness into me.
But now this sheriff thinks he's got a shot.
He wants to know where I'm headed, driving
so quick my touring car conjures a storm.
I'm the eye, touching what I damn well please.
Yes, even this girl, my girl, her pale skin,
just like my money, resting near my thigh.
I give it to him, his fifty buck fine,
pay him, then hit him again. He won't need
to swing out on my road another time.

FEAR

Do not change
your soap. I will not
know you. Fresh
from the shower
you smell sharp,
like a stone.
I know this.
I call it love.

Like my knowledge
of this hillside: sage
on the steepest slope,
eucalyptus
near the rocky caves. This is how
I find my way home.

CONTRABAND . . .

FARM BUREAU ADVISOR

They suggested that the man who taught them
not to choke fields with tight turns of growing
but to sometimes let them breathe as deeply
as uncorseted girls, the one black man
they ever knew the government to trust
with a job and a salary, the man
who lectured at the university
when few of them read further than their names
across a ledger, yes, they suggested
that Thornton's father must have forgotten
his place when he bought that new Ford model
and drove past town onto their country roads,
and they warned him: *A horse and cart will do
just fine next time you come around these parts.*

Free Masons at the Door

Every black Mason with a sugar jar
of savings had a little less money
after those two men knocked. Those tar-seared men.

Folks said in Cuba Negro men's faces
could hold their own shape. Despite their valise
full of bullets, what hope did these men have
unless they could get quickly to the docks?

Thornton Sr. had a truck and he drove
the Brothers to New Orleans. They all gave
what they could to help the men book passage.

Those bodies would heal, but no one could pluck
that furious feathered fluttering. If
they didn't leave, who could ever cut down
the high strung beating of those scarred men's hearts?

PREACHER WAS A STERN WOMAN'S SON

Thornton's mother blessed him with sense enough
to quit a church where worship meant women
loosening their stays; where they shouted, leapt,
and waved their hot fingers under God's nose.
His mother taught him: *Ladies hold hearts still.*

So the Sunday altos carried him, twice,
around the altar before the choir sat
to appraise him from behind, he resigned.

He had found no Mrs. yet. But he knew
the girl he wanted would never hug him
at Meeting like the Word had just primed her
for Friday night. She would not be like these
women, whose souls shook for the Rapture. Lord,
he couldn't stop them long enough for grace.

CHORE SONG

This is the house my great-grandmother built:

Twelve children, each with a task: the butcher,
the baker, the clothes-washing girl.

                                                    Grandma,
still a small-voiced child, learned her jobs: to sweep,
to dust, to make the beds inside that house
like a concerto.

                              The order set, chores
were lyric.

                      Eight pianos in that house.

And sometimes people playing every one.

Have you walked, lately, deep in the forest
when bird songs swell, each pitch raising the next?

Would you call that chaos?

                                Neither that house-
song, cleaner than the sparrow's.

                                Though God's eyes
were weak, his ears could surely light on them
perched there, outside that small and shuttered town.

At the Alpha Phi Alpha Ball

He warned her once and then a second time.
He'd torn one girl's dress, scuffed another's shoe
with his black sole. He had no ballroom legs
at all. But she'd had enough of talking
by the punch. Her eyes waltzed the body-dark
parquet, and he knew a third denial
would be far worse than tripping her brightness
across the floor. So Thornton took her hand.

The others had not learned patience teaching
brothers, five in all, to dance, but this girl
taught his arms where they belonged—his left hand
soft against her palm, his right hand dreaming
through fabric to her shoulder. She taught him
what it means to love a moving body.

ARK

I will enter you as hope enters me,
through blinding liquid, light of rain, and I
will stay inside until you send me out;
I will stay inside until you ground me.
We cannot outrun the rain. So many
summers I have tried. So many summers.
But when the rumble calls after the spark
there can be no escape. No outstripping
the drench soak, the wet sheath, the water caul.
This is more than you want to hear. Much more
than I want to tell you. Tabernacle
transporting my life from the desert, you,
the faith I am born and reborn into,
you, rescuer, deliverer of rain.

My Grandmother Takes
the Youth Group to Services

The sky's wide open blue told her, *Go in*
where you have never been before, and where
she went she took the children. Older girls
in long skirts, little black heels, white collars
rough with starch, and hair still hot from the comb,
along with boys their age, pants creased, shoes blacked
and bright. Little Linda in Topeka
had upset no one yet, but that black shock,
Lynchburg's largest high school class in years, did.

Surprised, the white minister welcomed her
with silence, but that evening his voice fumed
through Thornton's phone. *Your pretty wife should trust*
the good Lord's plan. Let her know, in heaven,
negroes will have to learn their rightful place.

The Preacher's Wife Speaks at the Dunbar High School Commencement

You are the crop that grows
wild tall. That, wicked brambled, twists
up, around, and over the lean poles
grounding you.

The plants that shoot and swing
in their eager-budding, lanky
way, you sway up
bright and juice full.

Sweet you write worlds globed
and green in such ways
as I have seen and others
I have not. Sometimes
in words like rich-soiled plots.

You are the bountiful crop.

Let the People Worship as They Will

During all those years watching their father
command from the pulpit, my mother learned
to venerate the still core of her faith
while her sister coveted the boarders'
and loose-lipped girls' license to call God down
into their rowdy hours.

                        Imagine them
before the altar, two sisters growing
apart. My mother bows, administers
a psalm. Her sister, tired of worshipping
a quick and quiet Lord, sings every verse
of her hymn, flushing silence from the flock.

Dresses the same, but faces different
as one key from the next, they march away
already, each toward her separate gate.

Book Smart

You would deny a man the chance to read
about the life of Christ? Thornton once asked
Lynchburg's librarian. She allowed him
to study in the basement after that.
For Thornton, learning meant growing nearer
to God. To worship with the intellect,
where intellect was contraband, proved faith.

Forty-five heat-whipped summers crawled across the States
before I found my way around Chicago
with a map borrowed from Granddad Thornton.
I'd made a new friend. We were past the limits
of her West Side block when she asked, *What's that*
water over there? The Ocean? I laughed.
I'd never known such ignorance before.

CLEANING

I learned regret at Mother's sink,
jarred tomatoes, river-mud brown,
a generation old, lumping
down the drain. Hating wasted space,
I had discarded what I could
not understand. I hadn't known
a woman to fight drought or frost
for the promise of winter meals,
hadn't known my great-grandmother,
or what it was to have then lose
the company of that woman
who, upon seeing her namesake,
child of her child, grown and gliding
into marriage, gifted the fruit
of her garden, a hard-won strike
against want. Opening the jar,
I knew nothing of the rotting
effect, the twisting grip of years
spent packing, of years spent moving,
further each time, from known comforts:
a grandmother's garden, her rows
always neat, the harvest: bright wealth
mother hoarded. I understood
only the danger of a date
so old. Understanding clearly
what is fatal to the body,
I only understood too late
what can be fatal to the heart.

The Preachers Eat Out

Vernon Johns

There were maybe four of them, perhaps five.
They were headed, where? It does not matter,
only, they were not home yet, were not near
anyone who could have cared. So hungry,
they stopped there anyway. And when they heard,
We don't serve your kind, one among them laughed,
That's okay. We're not hungry for our kind.
We've come for food. And when the one waitress
who would serve them—she had children at home
and these were tips—finished breaking their plates
behind the building, he called her over
to the table. *Lady, my one regret*
is that we don't have appetite enough
to make you break every damned plate inside this room.

Greyhound to Baton Rouge

Certainly they all understood the law,
but the white lady four rows from the front
and next to the one free seat took the child
and made the tired mother, *Sit right down.*

Arm around his wife, the new father stood,
relieved to see his baby still sleeping.
Small peace.

                    Sunday last he preached a story
like this. Remember Mary and Joseph
with their child? Do not forget they were chased
by the demands of one man.

                         The driver
surprised no one. *I will not move this bus,
you hear?* The colored bus he ordered came,
empty, just for them. *Go now. Take your wife.
Boy, get your baby out the lady's hands.*

SERVICE STATION, TENNESSEE

Even a man of God sometimes runs out
of prayers. But with his pretty wife and girls
there with him, all their bodies locked inside
that loose-rod car, Thornton couldn't think that
he might meet silence soon.

                    There was no one
who would help. Only six men hammering
their palms with wrenches, fixing other cars,
saying, *We'll get to you when we're through here.*

Then a kid on furlough from Korea,
where his own life was watched by Negro men,
tailed their car to Knoxville.

                    There was no choice.
The soldier warned him, *These are my people.*
Man, I know them. If you can move this car
at all, leave this town. Leave while you still can.

HOME GOING

They are old now, acquainted with silence.

Not the same boisterous congregation.

Only four sisters left alive,

                        the last
brother's curled limbs crumbling into the earth
they've just thrown down.

                     Still, they can remember
themselves, a pitch-strained quartet recalling
their choir's tune.

                  None younger than eighty,
all pictured here in frills and school-girl white,

these women do not have frown-torn faces.

Though their skin is light, their eyes weigh something
only they can measure.

                    The funeral
had just finished when my camera framed them
passing the time before being taken
some other place, hymn-singing, together.

After Applying to Harvard, Colgate, Yale

When the last letter came, reminding him
that he was black, Thornton's answering feat
left his country behind. With a Fulbright,
he sailed for England, and while out, pacing
the deck, he met the first white man whose eyes
he recognized. What couldn't that man hold?
For the first time, Thornton spoke easily
of his own life: his wife, his two small girls.
He recalled his book-walled home, the kingdom
he'd abdicated, the tower guards, men
who tried to keep him far from what he loved.

It's very hard to live a dream at home,
Thornton says he told the man, Prince Edward,
who understood, who'd loved, who'd also left.

WHAT TO EAT, AND WHAT TO DRINK, AND WHAT TO LEAVE FOR POISON

I.

Only now, in spring, can the place be named:
tulip poplar, daffodil, crab apple,
dogwood, budding pink-green, white-green, yellow
on my knowing. All winter I was lost.
Fall, I found myself here, with no texture
my fingers know. Then, worse, the white longing
that downed us deep three months. No flower heat.
That was winter. But now, in spring, the buds
flock our trees. Ten million exquisite buds,
tiny and loud, flaring their petalled wings,
bellowing from ashen branches vibrant
keys, the chords of spring's triumph: fisted heart,
dogwood; grail, poplar; wine spray, crab apple.
The song is drink, is color. Come. Now. Taste.

II.

The song is drink, is color. Come now, taste
what the world has to offer. When you eat
you will know that music comes in guises—
bold of crepe myrtle, sweet of daffodil—
beyond sound, guises they never told you
could be true. And they aren't. Except they are
so real now, this spring, you know them, taste them.
Green as kale, the songs of spring, bright as wine,
the music. Faces of this season grin
with clobbering wantonness—see the smiles
open on each branch?—until you, too, smile.
Wide carnival of color, carnival
of scent. We're all lurching down streets, drunk now
from the poplar's grail. Wine spray: crab apple.

III.

From the poplar's grail, wine spray. Crab apple
brightens jealously to compete. But by
the crab apple's deep stain, the tulip tree
learns modesty. Only blush, poplar learns,
lightly. Never burn such a dark-hued fire
to the core. Tulip poplar wants herself
light under leaf, never, like crab apple,
heavy under tart fruit. Never laden.
So the poplar pours just a hint of wine
in her cup, while the crab apple, wild one,
acts as if her body were a fountain.
She would pour wine onto you, just let her.
Shameless, she plants herself, and delivers,
down anyone's street, bright invitations.

IV.

Down anyone's street-bright invitations.
Suck 'em. Swallow 'em. Eat them whole. That's right,
be greedy about it. The brightness calls
and you follow because you want to taste,
because you want to be welcomed inside
the code of that color: red for thirst; green
for hunger; pink, a kiss; and white, stain me
now. Soil me with touching. Is that right?
No? That's not, you say, what you meant. Not what
you meant at all? Pardon. Excuse me, please.
Your hand was reaching, tugging at this shirt
of flowers and I thought, I guess I thought
you were hungry for something beautiful.
Come now. The brightness here might fill you up.

V.

Come. Now the brightness here might fill you up,
but tomorrow? Who can know what the next
day will bring. It is like that, here, in spring.
Four days ago, the dogwood was a fist
in protest. Now look. Even she unfurls
to the pleasure of the season. Don't be
ashamed of yourself. Don't be. This happens
to us all. We have thrown back the blanket.
We're naked and we've grown to love ourselves.
I tell you, do not be ashamed. Who is
more wanton than the dancing crepe myrtle?
Is she ashamed? Why, even the dogwood,
that righteous tree of God's, is full of lust
exploding into brightness every spring.

VI.

Exploding into brightness every spring,
I draw you close. I wonder, do you know
how long I've wanted to be here? Each year
you grasp me, lift me, carry me inside.
Glee is the body of the daffodil
reaching tubed fingers through the day, feeling
her own trumpeted passion choiring air
with hot, colored song. This is a texture
I love. This is life. And, too, you love me,
inhale my whole being every spring. Gone
winter, heavy clod whose icy body
fell into my bed. I must leave you, but
I'll wait through heat, fall, freeze to hear you cry:
Daffodils are up. My God, what beauty!

VII.

Daffodils are up, my God! What beauty
concerted down on us last night. And if
I sleep again, I'll wake to a louder
blossoming, the symphony smashing down
hothouse walls, and into the world: music.
Something like the birds' return, each morning's
crescendo rising toward its brightest pitch,
colors unfurling, petals alluring.
The song, the color, the rising ecstasy
of spring. My God. This beauty. This, this
is what I've hoped for. All my life is here
in the unnamed core—dogwood, daffodil,
tulip poplar, crab apple, crepe myrtle—
only now, in spring, can the place be named.

Biographical Note

Camille Dungy has received fellowships from the National Endowment for the Arts, The Virginia Commission for the Arts, Cave Canem, and the American Antiquarian Society, and she has been a John Atherton Scholar at the Bread Loaf Writers' Conference and a Tennessee Williams Scholar at the Sewanee Writer's Conference. Once the Writer-in-Residence at Rocky Mountain National Park, Dungy has also been awarded fellowships and residencies by the Norton Island/Eastern Frontier Society, The Corporation of Yaddo, the Virginia Center for the Creative Arts, and the Ragdale Foundation. A graduate of Stanford University and the University of North Carolina, Greensboro's MFA Program, Dungy is currently Associate Professor of Literature and Creative Writing at Randolph-Macon Woman's College in Lynchburg, Virginia. She is assistant editor of *Gathering Ground: A Reader Celebrating Cave Canem's First Decade* (University of Michigan Press, 2006).